surfing

surfing

by Larry Dane Brimner

A First Book

Franklin Watts
A Division of Grolier Publishing
New York   London   Hong Kong
Sydney   Danbury, Connecticut

No sport is completely risk-free. You should exercise caution and common sense if you decide to undertake surfing, and you should never surf beyond your ability. The author and publisher will take no responsibility or liability for injuries resulting from your attempts to surf.

Photographs ©: Corbis-Bettmann: 14; Outside Images/Peter Sterling: cover, 3, 10, 11, 17, 21, 22, 23, 24, 25, 26, 27, 29, 30, 31, 33, 35, 36, 37, 39,43, 44, 45, 47, 49, 50, 51, 52, 53, 54, 55.

Interior Design: Janice Noto-Helmers

Library of Congress Cataloging-in-Publication Data

Brimner, Larry Dane.
Surfing / by Larry Dane Brimner.
p. cm. — (A First book)
Includes bibliographical references and index.
Summary: Describes the history, equipment, and basic techniques of surfing, as well as safety issues and surfing etiquette.
ISBN 0–531–20315–8 (lib. bdg.)   0-531-15891-8 (pbk.)
1. Surfing—Juvenile literature. [1. Surfing.] I. Title. II. Series.
GV840.S8B75 1997
797.3'2—dc21   97–9428
                                                         CIP
                                                          AC

Contents

dedication

To the Dolores Public Library staff: Carole Arnold, Laurie Callaway, Shirley Dennison, Barbara Hamilton, and Rene Lushko-for helping me "surf" Colorado's libraries.

acknowledgements

The author is indebted to Rich Watkins of the California Surf Museum for answering questions and providing advice during the development of this book. His insight and knowledge helped to give it shape. Special thanks, also, to Mike Carter—fellow writer, artist, friend, and surfer—for taking time from his surfing schedule to check the manuscript for accuracy and for making suggestions.

CHAPTER ONE

A Sport of Kings

You shuttle along, skimming the sea's blue surface, white froth nipping at the tail of your surfboard. It is a delicate dance of surfer on sea. Balance. Precision. Timing. You won't win, of course. Not against the sea. The sea is a mighty and powerful adversary, and a capricious one. But, for a while at least, you and the sea are one — dancing, surging, and flowing together toward shore.

Surfing is as new as the latest advances in design and materials and as old as history. Although no one knows exactly when surfing began, historians credit the south Pacific islands as its birthplace — places that today are known as Tahiti, Bora Bora, and Hawaii. Long before Captain James Cook sailed into Hawaii's

8

Kealakekua Bay in 1778, island people had become proficient surf riders, as witnessed by Cook's first in command, Lieutenant James King. He offered the first published account of surfing:

> Sometimes 20 or 30 go without the Swell of the Surf, & lay themselves flat upon an oval piece of plank about their Size & breadth . . . they wait the time of the greatest Swell that sets on Shore, & altogether push forward with their Arms to keep on its top . . . & the great art is to guide the plank so as always to keep it in a proper direction on the top of the Swell.*

The early Hawaiians surfed using two main types of boards, the alaia and olo. The larger and thicker of these, the olo, could be seventeen feet long (5.2 m) or longer and weigh more than 150 pounds (68 kg). In appearance, both the alaia and olo resembled modern surfboards, but they did not have tail fins, or skegs.

Surfing was enjoyed by commoners and royalty alike, although the alii, or chiefly class, held the highest reputation for skill. Freed from everyday chores, they could pursue surfing with an unmatched devotion on special beaches set aside just for them. The skill they achieved on surfboards served to enhance their leadership position, since chiefs were expected to possess greater strength and stamina than commoners.

*Lt. King's unedited log, reprinted in the *Voyage of the Resolution and Discovery,* by John C. Beaglehole, 1967, and in *Surfing: A History of the Ancient Hawaiian Sport,* by Ben Finney and James D. Houston, 1996

By mastering monster waves like this one, Hawaiian royalty enhanced their leadership positions.

Surfing was both recreation and competition. Wagering on contests by contestants as well as spectators, by commoners as well as the alii, was a favorite pastime. At stake could be a canoe, fishing nets, or tapa cloth. Sometimes it was a chief's kingdom or a person's freedom.

Not all surfing contests pitted surfer against surfer. One type of contest was between a surfer and sled rider. In this contest, at the exact moment a surfer caught a wave and began moving toward a point on shore, an opponent would pitch a stone holua sled down a slope and ride it toward the same point. The first to reach the designated point was the winner.

This enthusiasm for surfing came to an end, however, with the arrival of Christian missionaries in 1820. The missionaries didn't approve of gambling and considered surfing without clothes or in a loincloth immoral. They impressed upon key rulers that surfing was against the laws of God, and surfing was nearly forgotten for one hundred years.

In the early 1900s, however, surfing was rediscovered. Although the few remaining surfers no longer used the large olo boards and their skills were rudimentary compared to those that Lieutenant King had witnessed in the 1700s, the sport captured the imagination of visitors. Among those visitors was Jack London, one of the most popular authors of the time. In 1907, he wrote an impassioned article about surfing called "A Royal Sport: Surfing at Waikiki"—the equivalent to promoting the sport on MTV today.

Still, surfing may have remained a Hawaiian sport if it weren't for the Pacific Electric Railroad, which was pushing its tracks into southern California. Ticket sales were sluggish, so the railroad hired George Freeth, an ace Hawaiian surfer, to introduce the public to ocean sports. At about the same time that London was penning his article, Freeth, who was billed as "the man who could walk on water," was offering surfing classes to youngsters and performing his wave-riding skills for audiences at Redondo Beach, the terminus for the railroad. Surfing, once again, became the rage.

Five years later, in 1912, Hawaiian-born Duke Paoa Kahanamoku stopped in southern California on his way to the Olympics. He barnstormed up and down the coast with his solid redwood board and astounded crowds with his surfing skill. He went on to win an Olympic gold medal in swimming in the 100-meter freestyle. Today he is known as the grandfather of modern Hawaiian surfing.

Quickly adopted by ocean-minded high school and college students, surfing was on its way to becoming a national and international pastime. In Australia, surfing was spurred on by its integration with the Surf Life Saving Association, which was begun in 1907. When Kahanamoku toured there in 1915, surfboard riding was seen to have a natural tie-in to surf safety and rescue.

Although surfing had always been enjoyed by both men and women, the modern version was male dominated. Still, women were not to be outdone by men. In 1925, Faye Baird Fraser became the first documented modern woman surfer when, using a 90-pound (41-kg) surfboard, she "shot the pier" along a San Diego, California, beach. Shooting the pier, or riding between a

Duke Paoa Kahanamoku, swimmer and legendary surfer.

pier's pilings, is something only the most skilled surfers can do without mishap. (*It is not a recommended activity!*) Fraser played down her accomplishment, saying that it was unintentional, that she was just trying to hold on to a surfboard that was hurtling toward the pier.

Whether or not she planned it, her success was an indication that women, as well as men, could master the art and sport of surfing. Today, most surfing contests have women's divisions, and the Women's International Surfing Association represents their interests.

In the 1950s and 1960s, a spate of beach movies increased the popularity of surfing and created the image of the surfer-rebel. Interest in the sport seemed to decline during the Vietnam era but surged again in the late 1980s and 1990s. Today, interest in surfing is so widespread that it is not limited to states, provinces, and countries with beachfronts. Technology has intervened, and wave machines now produce "surf" on artificial lakes in the desert and on the plains. And everywhere—from New Mexico to New South Wales, from Beverly Hills to Biarritz—kids adopt the "surfer look," whether they ever venture onto a surfboard or not.

CHAPTER TWO

Basic Equipment

Surfing has two basic requirements: a surfboard and a wave.

Today's surfboards are miracles of technology and ingenuity. Built from molded foam and fiberglass, they are lightweight—25 pounds (11 kg) or less—and easy to carry. They generally range in length from about 5 to 6 feet (1.5 to 1.8 m), although some surfers are returning to "long boards" for the challenge of riding them. Modern long boards measure from 7 feet 6 inches to 9 feet 6 inches (2.3 to 2.9 m); occasionally, you may spot the 11-foot (3.4-m) variety popular in the 1960s. Why do surfers choose one over the other? Short boards offer an experienced surfer greater maneuverability than long boards, and this is an essential trait for "hot-dogging"—performing fancy moves—during competition. Long boards, however, offer more stability on bigger, faster waves.

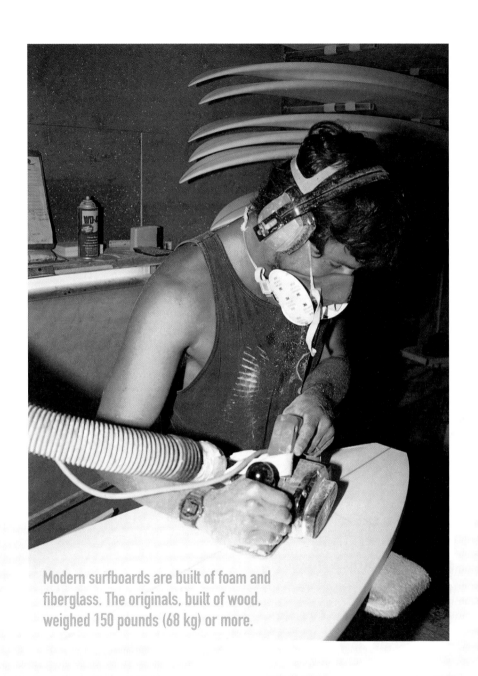

Modern surfboards are built of foam and fiberglass. The originals, built of wood, weighed 150 pounds (68 kg) or more.

Modern surfboards have tail fins called skegs. Older surfboard designs have a single skeg, but the trend and industry standard is for three skegs, called "thrusters," that are offset for greater turning and performance ability. The three-skeg design was an innovation of Australian Simon Anderson in 1981. The skegs are arranged differently for specific surf conditions and desired performance results. The beginning surfer doesn't need to worry about fin arrangements. Just make sure your first board has at least one.

Modern surfboards are a far cry from those used by the ancient Hawaiians. It seems that as interest in surfing grew, so did complaints about the weight of the boards. The original alaia and olo boards were built of heavy hardwoods, such as mahogany or koa wood. The modern surfboard is a result of experimentation in both Hawaii and California. Tom Blake, a mainlander who surfed in Hawaii, is credited with being the first serious surfboard designer. "Mainlander" is what Hawaiians call a person who is from the North American continent, especially the contiguous United States. Blake hollowed out the basic olo design in 1926 and gave the tail a pronounced point. Built of pine or redwood, his "cigar boxes," as they were called, were 40 to 50 pounds

(18 to 23 kg) lighter than solid boards and popular with novice surfers from Hawaii to California into the 1950s.

Some say Blake was also the first to introduce a skeg, but others say that innovation belongs to California surfers. Whatever the facts, the addition of a skeg was an important advance in design. A tail fin prevented side slipping on steep waves and put the surfer more in control of the surfboard.

Innovations that were clearly the product of California surfers and designers include experimenting with balsa and fiberglass boards. Balsa wood surfboards had been tried during the 1930s and 1940s, and failed. Balsa was too porous and fragile. Covering balsa boards with fiberglass strengthened and waterproofed them. They became so popular in Malibu, California, that they acquired the moniker "Malibu boards." The "scoop nose," still used on modern surfboards, helped to keep a board from "submarining," or dropping nose first into a wave. A "rocker line," or slight curvature from nose to tail, produced a faster and more responsive board.

The Right Surfboard

Today's professional surfers are probably still searching for the perfect surfboard. But since they haven't found it, they typically use different boards for different waves. A beginning surfer, however, should look for a long board—one that is at least as tall as your hand raised above your head. A long board will provide more buoyancy, making it easier for you to balance, and will be easier for you to maneuver. Look for a board that is thick—around 3 inches (7.6 cm)—and wide—about 22 inches (56 cm) in the middle.

The best way to experiment with different boards is to rent them from a local surf shop. Don't buy the first thing you see or ride. Seek the advice of shop clerks. Most people who work in surf shops are experienced surfers and will be able to make recommendations. Admit that you're a beginner. The clerk will respect your honesty and be better able to point you toward a potentially suitable board. When you've found the board that feels right, you'll know it. Then you can purchase a board that is similar or have one custom designed.

Other Equipment

The surfboard you rent or purchase should have a leash. A leash is an elastic cord that attaches to the tail of the surfboard on one end and to your ankle on the other. It prevents the board from flying helter-skelter toward

A young surfer gets his beginning on a long, wide board in shallow water.

Wipe outs are often dramatic, but can pose danger. It is wise to protect your head when thrown from a board. The leash will prevent a "killer board."

shore when you wipe out, or fall off, and everybody eventually wipes out. An out-of-control surfboard can be a dangerous thing—so dangerous that one is called a "killer board."

You will also need wax. Wax is rubbed onto the deck of the surfboard (the side you stand on) to give the surfer better traction when in the water. Although you may not want to purchase one the very first time you go surfing, most surfers today wear neoprene wet suits. A wet suit will definitely give you the "surfer look," and it will help keep you warm.

A wet suit's snug fit allows a little water to enter the suit, where it is warmed by your body and insulates you from the colder water outside. Many surfers wear a thin nylon shirt under their wet suits to prevent friction rash to their necks and underarms. Of course, if you plan to surf in 75° F water (24° C water), you probably won't require a wet suit.

In warm water, surfers abandon their wet suits.

The Right Waves

You can't surf without ridable waves. It's a fact of surfing.

The primary source of waves is wind. When wind agitates the water, a wave-form begins to roll toward shore in much the same way that ripples fan out when

a pebble is dropped in a pond. As the wave-form, or swell, enters shallow water along a coast, ridable waves begin to form when the wave back overtakes the wave front.

A wave breaks in one of two main ways: it plunges or it spills. A plunging wave leaps out at the shore, often forming a water tunnel, or tube. Plungers are spectacular but more hazardous for the surfer. A spilling wave, on the other hand, is gentler. It crumbles down the wave face and allows a surfer to keep ahead of the breaking foam.

The right waves for a beginning surfer are spillers. And not giant spillers either! Waves that are waist-high or less are ideal to learn on. All you need is a wave that breaks and has a little push, and you'll be ready to surf.

A shallow, spilling wave such as this is ideal for a beginner.

CHAPTER THREE

Avoiding Injury

Assuming that it is more active than playing chess, any sport carries a certain amount of risk when you decide to participate. Surfing is no different. But there are things that any surfer can do to reduce the chances of injury.

Surfing is a water sport. The very first thing a surfer should know is how to swim. If you don't know how to swim, learn. Not only should you know *how* to swim, but you should also feel *confident* in your ability to swim from point A to point B.

The United States Surfing Association (USSA), an early surfing organization and precursor to the United States Surfing Federation, recommended that a beginning surfer be able to swim 100 yards (91 m) at full strength and 500 yards (457 m) at a controlled pace. It is still good advice today. You should build your stamina before attempting to surf because surfing is a rigorous sport. The USSA also recommended that

Nobody surfs without wiping out. Really!

you be able to tread water for 20 minutes and then swim 100 yards (91 m). Your ability to act sensibly and confidently in the water could help save your life or, perhaps, the life of another.

A smart surfer will never surf alone. Surf with a buddy or close enough to other surfers that they might help should trouble develop. Also, it is a smart move for beginners to surf in an area with lifeguards on duty.

Every year, some surfers get in trouble when their leashes become entangled in lobster traps. Stay out of lobstering areas. No matter how good the surf, it just isn't worth the risk.

Rocky cliffs test an experienced surfer's skills, but they should be avoided by the beginner.

If you become caught in a rip current, a strong current that pulls you out to sea, keep your head. Don't paddle against it. If you do, you'll soon exhaust yourself. Instead, paddle *across* it, more or less parallel to the beach. When you pop out of the rip current, paddle toward shore.

Remember that you're a beginner. You don't need giant breakers to practice and perfect your skills. If anything, monster surf will prove frustrating to a beginner. For the time being, restrict yourself to reasonable surf—waves that are breaking at about waist high or smaller.

Surf adjacent to a wide, sandy beach. Waves that break on reefs and rocky cliffs offer experienced surfers unique challenges, but they may spell disaster for the beginner.

Always be in control of your surfboard. A loose board is a

danger to others as well as to yourself. Wear a leash. And hold on to your board if you can. If you wipe out—and chances are that you will—stay alert for the tug of your surfboard against the leash. Shield yourself in the direction of the tug. If you don't feel a tug, the board may be directly above you. Cover your head with your hands as you resurface.

Wiping out is a fact of surfing. When it happens to you, fall away from the impact zone—where the lip of the wave lands—and away from the trajectory of your surfboard.

Every year, surfers experience head injuries when they fall headfirst into water that was shallower than they thought. When you fall, cover your head with your hands.

Safety First

Be alert.

Obey lifeguard warnings and restrictions.

Surf away from swimmers.

Don't surf alone or at night.

If you wipe out, try to grab the leash as close to the surfboard as possible.

If you find yourself on a collision course with another surfer, sink the tail of your board and end your run.

If you are bleeding or experience cramping, get out of the water.

Become familiar with first aid, especially artificial respiration.

CHAPTER FOUR

Playing It Cool

Individual sports, such as surfing, sometimes seem to lack the organization and rules of team sports. While competitive events are organized by the Association of Surfing Professionals and other organizations, an ordinary day of surfing at your local beach doesn't have to operate under any set of "rules." This was fine in the 1950s when the number of surfers was relatively small and everyone had a chance to catch a wave. Today, the number of surfers is staggering, and there aren't always enough good waves to go around. To provide a hint of order to a crowded surfing lineup, there is an unwritten code of courtesy that most surfers abide by.

Surfers "line up" to wait for a wave.

In a nutshell, the code favors experience and local-ism. That is, a beginning surfer will give an experienced surfer first crack at a wave. Similarly, a local has more right to catch a wave than does a visitor. Given those limitations, the code says that the surfer who catches a wave closest to its peak is entitled to that wave.

As a beginner, you probably won't know who is experienced or who is local. The best tactic is to hang back a while and observe. See who the other surfers are yielding to and do the same. Demonstrate respect for those other surfers already in the lineup, especially to those the others are yielding to, and they'll likely return it by allowing you to catch a wave or two. Come into a lineup as a wet-behind-the-ears upstart, though, and you might get snaked, or cut off by someone with greater skill. Although snaking another surfer isn't appropriate behavior—a beginner should never snake another surfer—this tactic is sometimes used to signal to novices that they need to show respect to the experienced surfers in the lineup.

It is also considered good form to join a lineup, or group of waiting surfers, at the edge of the cluster. Never paddle out to the middle of a lineup. It's like taking cuts in line, and it's sure to draw the ire of those already there. Even worse, paddling into the middle of a lineup will probably put you in the way of some-

Stay to the edge of the line-up when paddling out.

body's perfect ride. Interrupt an experienced surfer's perfect ride and you'll find out what real anger is—if you're not smacked in the head by the nose of a rocketing surfboard first! Play it cool. Paddle out to the periphery. It's safer there. It's saner there. And you'll be demonstrating that you have respect for the others in the lineup.

Finally, you should always be aware. Know who's in front of you, behind you, and to either side of you. If somebody takes off to catch a wave, try to stay out of the way. They may return the favor some day.

Surfing lineups are a strange hierarchy. But beginners who take the time to study them and who show a good attitude toward the system won't go unnoticed. They will be the ones rewarded with waves of their very own.

Eventually, even beginners will be given a chance to catch a wave if they show respect to the "locals."

CHAPTER FIVE

Catching Your First Waves

Once you have a surfboard, you'll probably be eager to test your skills on water. But the best way to get started is to practice pop-ups on dry land first. A pop-up is the act of standing up—going from the prone paddling position to standing upright on the board. It's a maneuver that begins and ends in a flash. It combines a slight push-up with a swinging motion of the feet, so that you go from lying to standing in one smooth movement. Some beginners add an extra movement by going to one knee before standing. Don't do this! It is bad surfing form, and a bad habit that is difficult to break. Observe the surfers in the water as they pop-up. See how fluid the movement is for them. This is the form you want to emulate. And practice, practice, practice.

You can practice pop-ups on a beached surfboard— watch out for the tail fin—or simply on the sand. This is when you'll discover if you are regular-footed or

A regular-footed surfer demonstrates the pop-up.

39

goofy-footed. If you are regular-footed, you'll stand with your left foot forward. If you are goofy-footed, you'll stand with your right foot forward. No matter which foot you lead with, stand with your toes angled slightly toward the front of the surfboard. Your back foot will be approximately perpendicular to the board's length. It is the back foot that you'll attach the leash to when you're ready to venture into the water. Position your feet a bit wider than your shoulders and take a slightly crouched, knees-bent stance. Your arms will be outstretched for balance. This is the regular stance. With actual experience in the water, you'll probably modify it slightly to suit your own needs. Once your dry-land pop-up movement is smooth and fluid, you'll be ready to paddle out and try it in water.

Before paddling out, you'll want to wax your board. If you're using a rented board, it may have wax on it. It may even have gobs of wax on it. If this is the case, you'll have to scrape off the excess with a wax comb. If it isn't waxed or there are bare spots where you'll be standing, rub on some wax with long, even strokes until it begins to form beads. Be sure to apply wax to the side areas where you'll be placing your hands. Don't worry about waxing the front quarter of the board; you won't be standing there. Also, if your board has strips of grip tape on the deck, don't apply wax over them. Grip tape is sometimes used toward the rear of a board to give a surfer's back foot more traction for kick turns. Since wax melts, you'll want to keep the deck turned away from the sun when you're not in the water.

Paddling Out

Some surfers say that most surfing time is spent paddling. This may come as a surprise to you if your notion of surfing is limited to riding waves. But if you think about it, it makes sense. In order to ride waves, a surfer must first reach them, and this is usually accomplished by paddling out to them and then by paddling to catch them. Then the process begins again. Other surfers argue that waiting consumes most of their time. Either way, the amount of time surfers actually spend riding waves is a small percentage of their time on the board.

Before paddling out, study the surf. Even experienced surfers study the wave action before entering the water. Try to determine if there's a pattern to the waves. Usually waves come in sets followed by a lull, a quiet period when there are no waves. It makes sense to wait for a lull before paddling out because then you won't have to expend as much energy fighting through breaking waves. As you study the surf, also take note of where the other surfers are. You'll want to paddle out on the edges of the surfing area to where the waves are just breaking. Keep in mind that a person riding a wave has the right of way. In the beginning, stay closer to shore. When you gain experience, skill, and confidence, you can join the lineup a little farther out.

Although some surfers like to paddle out in a kneeling position, it is easier if you lie flat on the board. To make progress, keep your board "in trim," or balanced. If you lie too far forward on your board, its nose will dive under the water. This is called "pearling." No progress there. If you're too far back, the nose will periscope and you'll stall. No progress there, either. You'll soon learn where to position yourself to remain in trim. Stroke by stroke, paddle directly into the oncoming swells.

If a wave breaks in front of you, aim your board directly into the white water. Surfers call the white water "soup." Grip the rails, or sides, of your surfboard as you meet the soup and do a slight push-up. This offers the least resistance to the rush of water, allowing it to flow around you instead of pushing you all the way back to shore. As soon as you slip into the trough behind the wave, resume paddling.

By ducking under a wave, this surfer avoids being pushed back to shore when paddling out.

Another way to tackle a breaking wave when you're paddling out is to do a "duck dive." Before the soup hits you, scoot forward on your board, wrap your legs around it, and hold on to the rails. Then dive down with the nose of your board and let the wave roll over you.

When you surface, quickly scoot back and resume paddling.

An advanced surfer rides the wall of a wave.

"Catching" a Wave

You may picture yourself skimming along the wall of a wave, turning this way and that, the breaking wave never quite catching you. The "wall" is that part of a wave that is smooth and unbroken, the part before it breaks. The reality is that most people learn to surf in the white water that appears after a wave has broken. White water is easier to catch.

Some experienced surfers say that beginners should learn to catch a swell and to ride the wall from the very start because this is what you'll want to do when your skills develop. Perhaps this is true. But, as mentioned earlier, the soup is easier to catch. It is also less frustrating because you'll probably have more opportunity to practice and experiment in the soup than on the wall. Also, because experienced surfers don't bother with the soup, you'll tend to stay out of their way if you practice there. They'll like you for that. You'll have to determine what is best for you. Just keep in mind that you should never attempt to surf beyond your abilities.

Whether you are trying to catch a swell or ride in the soup, you'll want to begin paddling toward shore before your targeted wave actually reaches you. Knowing exactly when to begin paddling will come with experience, but generally you'll take off when the wave is about 10 to 15 feet (3 to 4.6 m) behind you. When the wave begins to pick you up and thrust you along, slide back and trim your board. Since keeping your board in trim, without pearling or stalling, is the key to successful surfing, you should practice this a few times before attempting to ride standing up.

When you get good at catching the wave and shooting in with your board in trim, you can try popping up.

Angling across a swell gets the most ride out of a wave.

Pop up just as you did in your dry-land practices. *Voila!* You're surfing.

And then you'll probably fall off. When you fall, try to hold on to your surfboard. If you can't, cover your head and fall away from it.

Feel for the tug against the leash. Remember, if there's no tug, protect your head as you resurface.

Now paddle out and try it again and again and again.

CHAPTER SIX

Wave Riding

Learning to surf is like learning to walk. It's relatively uncomplicated once you've mastered it, but you forget that you suffered myriad spills before that mastery came. Yet, just as you mastered walking, you'll master surfing. All it takes is practice and patience—and a bit of balance. Before you know it, you'll find yourself standing on a surfboard and riding a wave, taking a walk on water just like George Freeth. Bravo!

Angling and the Leaning Turn

When you did your observation from shore, you probably noticed that the surfers were riding toward the left or right, rather than straight in to the beach. This is called angling. By angling your surfboard, you'll get a longer ride. Paddling back out to the lineup also won't be so tedious because you'll end your ride before going all the way to shore.

You'll decide to angle left or right depending on which direction the wave is breaking. From your position on the surfboard looking toward shore, if the wave is breaking from right to left, you have a "left-hander." You'll angle your board toward the left. If the wave is breaking from left to right, it's a "right-hander," and you'll angle to the right. A closed-out wave breaks all at once and cannot be surfed. It is usually easier for a regular-footed surfer to surf "facing the wave," or to the left, and for a goofy-footed one to surf to the right.

A surfer catches a right-hander.

Begin angling your board when you are paddling to catch the wave. As the wave picks you up, pop up as you did before. Your goal is to keep your surfboard just ahead of the breaking wave. Keep your board in trim, and turn by shifting your weight and leaning. If you are regular-footed (left-foot forward), you'll turn right by shifting your weight to the balls of your feet. To turn left, shift your weight to your heels. Use your outstretched arms to maintain your balance.

Rear Foot Turns

The next turn you'll add to your repertoire is the rear foot turn. It's another basic turn, but slightly different from the leaning turn. To turn left using the rear foot turn, the rear foot is moved slightly back and to the left of your board if you are regular-footed. At the same time, shift your weight to your front foot. To turn right, move your back foot to the right side of the board and shift your weight to the front foot.

You may have trouble keeping your balance at first, but don't give up. Both kinds of turns will come naturally to you with practice.

To look like the professionals you see on the competitive circuit, you'll take the basic moves and refine them. Practice, practice, practice—until every move is smooth. You'll add cutbacks, roller coasters, and aerials to your repertoire, personalizing them with your own style. And you'll get more adventurous, trying out waves that a beginner should never consider and, eventually, riding the tube, the ultimate experience for any surfer. All of these are advanced moves that began with popping up and keeping a surfboard in trim, that began with mastering turning left and right. Believe it or not, the men and women you see competing in the World Championship Tour sponsored by the Association of Surfing Professionals were once beginners, too.

A rear-foot turn is slightly more advanced than a leaning turn, but still a basic technique.

Riding the tube—the ultimate experience for any surfer!

Publications and Organizations

You may want to know more about the sport of surfing. There are numerous magazines and books that will give you pointers, talk about the latest innovations, and describe the moves that champion surfers are using to win competitions.

Magazines

Surfer

Surfer Publications, Inc.
PO Box 1028
Dana Point, CA 92629

Surfing Magazine

PO Box 3010
San Clemente, CA 92025

Longboard Magazine

419 Main Street, Suite 158
Huntington Beach, CA 92648

Books

Evans, Jeremy. *Surfing*. New York: Crestwood House, 1993.

Finney, Ben, and Houston, James D. Surfing: *A History of the Ancient Hawaiian Sport*. San Francisco: Pomegranate Artbooks, 1996.

Gutman, Bill. *Surfing*. Minneapolis, Minn.: Capstone Press, 1995.

Madison, Arnold. *Surfing: Basic Techniques*. New York: David McKay, 1979.

Nentl, Jerolyn. *Surfing*. Mankato, Minn.: Crestwood House, 1978.

Werner, Doug. *Surfer's Start-Up: A Beginner's Guide to Surfing*. Chula Vista, Calif.: Tracks Publishing, 1993.

If you are a traveler, there are also surfing museums that you may want to put on your itinerary. Here are some of them.

California Surf Museum
223 North Coast Highway
Oceanside, CA 92054

C Street Surfing Museum
342 S. California Street
Ventura, CA 93001

Huntington Beach International Surfing Museum
411 Olive Street
Huntington Beach, CA

Several organizations promote competitive surfing events for adults and young people. Here are the main ones.

Association of Surfing Professionals (ASP)
PO Box 309
Huntington Beach, CA 92648

International Surfing Association (ISA)
Administrative World Headquarters
Surf Coast Plaza
PO Box 230
Torquay, Australia 3228

National Scholastic Surfing Association (NSSA)
PO Box 495
Huntington Beach, CA 92648

United States Surfing Federation (USSF)
7104 Island Village Drive
Long Beach, CA 90803

Women's International Surfing Association (WISA)
PO Box 512
San Juan Capistrano, CA 92693

Internet Resources

Because of the changeable nature of the Internet, sites appear and disappear very quickly. These resources offered useful information on surfing at the time of publication. Internet addresses must be entered with capital and lower-case letters exactly as they appear.

Yahoo!
http://www.yahoo.com/

The *Yahoo!* directory on the World Wide Web is an excellent place to find Internet sites on any topic.

SURFERmag.com
www.surfermag.com

This is the online version of *Surfer Magazine.* This site includes articles, photos, and MPEG movies related to surfing and features an online shop for buying surfing gear. This site also offers a forum for discussing surfing issues and provides links to other surfing resources.

US Open of Surfing

http://www.usopenofsurfing.com/

This site is maintained by the US Open of Surfing, a national surfing competition. The site offers discussion forums, a media center, image and MPEG galleries, and results and scores from the contests.

Surf Check

http://www.surfcheck.com/

This site features images of popular California surf spots updated daily at 6:00 am. Surf Check also offers tidal information, swell forecasts, and marine data of interest to California surfers.

The Complete Surfing Guide for Coaches

http://www.blackmagic.com/ses/book/toc.html

This site is an online version of the book *The Complete Surfing Guide for Coaches, Including Historical Notes* by famous surfer Bruce Gabrielson. Although the site is geared toward coaches, it includes a useful section on learning to surf and offers additional interesting information.

Index

About the Author

Larry Dane Brimner has written many First Books for Franklin Watts, including *Surfing, Rock Climbing, Mountain Biking, Karate,* and *Rolling . . . In-line.* He is also the author of several Watts books for older readers, including *Letters to Our Children*, and *Voices from the Camps: Internment of Japanese*  *Americans During World War II.* When he isn't writing, Mr. Brimner visits elementary schools throughout the country to discuss the writing process with young authors and readers.